C000055846

Photo by James Noir

John Darwin lives in Prestwich, North Manchester. His poetry show *Happy Hour* won the Best Spoken Word Performance Award at the Greater Manchester Fringe Festival 2021. This is his second collection with Flapjack Press.

By the author

Misery Begins at Home [1]
Holding Your Hand Through Hard Times [2]
The People's Republic of Poetry [2]
I Meet Myself Returning
Ultrasilence

[1] Published by Rubberybubberyboy Parchment
[2] With A Firm of Poets, published by Ossett Observer

JOHN DARWIN
ultrasilence

Flapjack Press

flapjackpress.co.uk
Exploring the synergy between performance and the page

Published in 2022 by Flapjack Press
Salford, Gtr Manchester
⊕ flapjackpress.co.uk **f** Flapjack Press
🐦 FlapjackPress ▶ Flapjack Press

ISBN 978-1-8384703-6-4

Cover photo by Leif Christoph Gottwald on Unsplash
⊕ unsplash.com/@project2204

Printed by Imprint Digital
Exeter, Devon
⊕ digital.imprint.co.uk

FSC

MANCHESTER
A UNESCO City
of Literature

For my brother, Gareth.
Son of my father.

Contents

A version of 'After Collyhurst Road' was first published in *The People's Republic of Mancunia* by Rik Jundi et al, ed. P. Neads [Flapjack Press, 2020], 'Open the door' in *Prole, Poetry and Prose #32*, eds. B. Evans & P. Robertson [Prole Books, 2021], 'The way that she left' and 'Statue of you' in *The Anthology of Tomorrow*, ed. P. Neads [Flapjack Press, 2019].

I have written a book about the complexity of human relationships.
We are all a little strange.
Some of the themes are uncomfortable and seldom acknowledged.
The older I become, the more confused I am.
Thanks for reading.

John Darwin
August 2022

Ultrasilence

It starts with the cowlick curl of oils

The layers of an undiscovered Van Gogh
each knife cut and brush stroke visible
but unnamed

Colour and texture melded
impasto

Sharp blue
knife cut and whipped to a point
for the teeter of anticipated sex

the titter of the aftermath
the salt sea air drifting in
through banging windows

Daubed sunrise yellow
flattened and fattened by the knife
for the absent courage
not needed at the start
arriving too late

Vermilion, zinc white, raw sienna
flicked in corners
barely seen by the casual observer
for the reigning confusion
the tears that rain

A badly drawn cow
Carl Smith, Reception Class 1
is how it ends

In the lee of the hill
the mizzle of Mossley
where dads don't explain
why mothers leave early

from unfeathered nests
leaving kids without nurture
for the scratch of the branch
and scars unacknowledged

Girls named as heroines
of old melodramas
Catherine, Rebecca
and someone or another

There's nothing as sad
as a child
with no mother

Turning right from the ginnel
past the petrol station
mist licked the tarmac
like the devil's tongue

On the top road
what appeared as roadkill
was a thrown stole
blown from a stolen car

discarded recklessly
by a Mancunian Isadora

Four miles south
the sun peeps over tall buildings

Barely skyscrapers
but distance lends romance

I won't be home for breakfast

Avoiding Simon

Prestwich precinct: a sixties construction common to many towns, where faces are familiar and some are to be avoided.

Every day is Saturday
A nightingale sings in the precinct

Strolling through piss alley
breath held tight

Tribute band dregs mingle
sporting oversized shiny Primark

pulling on fags and draw
same as the week before

past waste plastic, turning left
through showers of

snowdrop, crocus, tulip
white, yellow, red

bad council sculptures
the infamous water feature

another shattered shelter

Avoiding Simon
He's lost his head

The New Road is an early morning home for grounded pigeons and magpies picking at last night's discarded chips.

By the shop of beards and expensive lentils for displaced BBC hopefuls, the pub door crumbling lintel, charity shops with five-pound bargain jackets, Bus-Stop-Darren asks for a smoke.

Opposite, the crack-of-dawn newsagent puffs his cheeks, greets the early morning mitherer reluctantly, passes him yesterday's butties with a grin.

Slim chance of a lottery win.

Prospects dim as the half-light over Junction 17 gives way to sleet, wind, then baubles of snow sticking to the suicide prevention fence.

One last grip before she slips.

Hatted with a taupe tea cosy
scraping over-sized shoes
dragging a mauve wheeled suitcase
through the precinct of

pigeon spikes and early closed bank
"It's a friendly face thing"
says the toothy model in the window
"Banking on your terms"

He trawls through Cancer Research
All Aboard and Headway
for valuable gems

The felted hat from Georgian times
Elizabethan *Beano* annuals
a floaty chemise
from Napoleonic France

Henry's pewter tankard

A cracked cup –

Papal Visit 1982

Soil shod from soles
by watering can
yard swept speckless
in preparation

Soft cloth between
thumb and finger
forms a point to lick
the grain of leather
with healing cream

Tongue out concentration
or a Player's Navy Cut
ash often drooping
half-tippled
never falling

Shone with horse hair
brushed with love
oak box of implements
and ointments

snapped shut
held secure
with clean brass clips

They jump from bridges round here
get blamed for delaying the traffic
tie blooms to the railings
and leave them to wither
to remind us we die if we need to remember

Three days for the flowers to wilt
one less in the swelt of the summer
Deadheads bow brown
in a semblance of grief
for the blood and bone bedlam that played out beneath

They name bars after illness round here
like it's funny how many go Cuckoo
In a town full of locals that self-medicate
the CPN made her referral too late

In estate agents' bluster it isn't made clear
they jump from bridges round here

Turning left down Collyhurst Road
two miles to Albert Square
where auntie Mags is drinking
in the tavern
noon 'til night

Feeding birds
with two bob tubs of seeds
Hugh rolls his sleeves
leans on the lamppost
smiling

Grandma casts a shadow
hissing through bad teeth
"Feeding birds for money
you get what you deserve"

Lobbing crumbs for pigeons
a piece for each regret
of why he left for whisky
or the sea

and we all set sail up Collyhurst Road
in a Black Mariah van

Late afternoon on Market Street
HMV still selling LPs
a bad one-man band in the mid-autumn frown
a homeless girl perched on her knees

pleading for cash for a fix or a bite
a grin, or the sign of a hug
Tired of the scowls, the toss-eyed smirks
the tuts and the pitiful shrugs

I dipped in the pub down the steps to the left
a name I can't remember
before or after football
in a skint and grey November

Up the steps, half a dozen pints in
on a Manchester Saturday night
I had small need for comfort
and no stomach for a fight

The homeless girl had disappeared
but her sleeping bag remained
her bed was drizzle-sodden
the pavement dog-shit stained

There was someone proselytising
got lost in the push and shove
I'm not looking for Jesus
she was looking for love

I stole your Mars bar when I was six
Too good to resist

You had Brontë sister curls
You were rich

You left it unguarded
I trousered it

Lisa, I stole your Mars when I was six
I'm so fucking sorry

it wasn't a Twix

Gift

No jobs for engineers
in plastics extrusion

The 3-Day Week
no more Saturday cakes

Christmas 1972
no Raleigh Chopper

Posh kids on Buxton Close
didn't have my father

We were netting for starfish
grazing knees and toes on rocks
burning oil-splashed skin
in sun-soaked pools

playing cricket on flat sands
with the local we called Ray
and uncle Peter
unrelated

telling Illingworth jokes
Ray didn't understand
but a catch was a catch
on the warm Welsh sand

Faded prints
show deep-tanned skin
strange blond locks
lightly-belted swimmers

melted cheese in Tupperware
dirty babies' nappies
young, lithe, joyful parents

Holidays for beginners

If you take all my keys
lock the garage doors tight
cook my mind whisky-devilled
so I'm blind to your charms

If you dress your skin deep
with musk, lust and jewels
sing subtle, mind-bending
subliminal tunes

If you wake in the night
and the bed is still warm
but my body has gone
and my shoes have gone too

I've escaped on the mower
ten miles into town
and I'm drunk at the bar
where I'm drinking

You were in the queue at M&S
chatting to the check-out man
boring him softly
about the asparagus season

It was the fall of your hair

You were in the park
walking a dog like the one
that pissed on my shoes
the time you invited me home

It was the shape of your gait

You were lurking at the tram stop
whispering about
some abandoned boy in 1989

you understood the cruel
but didn't know the kind

The whisper barely audible
bar the accent of a bumpkin

it was the curve of your behind
and my unfair assumptions

Before the hipster influx
you were straightened but content
Now swamped by young achievers
with their child seat four-by-fours

Your once smart home is flaking
from chimney to foundation
A gentle wolf could
blow it to the ground

You shuffle from the door
to your twelve-year-old Fiesta
Your clothes are hanging off you
black and flecked with dust

You could be Frank and Margaret
Peregrine and Jean
Dorothy and Benjamin
Christopher and Joan

but you dance with vim
when the door is shut
joy-whisk 'round the room

Miles Davis tooting
on the gramophone

Had a bad day at work
Spun too many clichés
on the back of my hand
I told and did not show
rhymed badly without
reference to meaning
Left my girlfriend, wept

Had a bad day at work
Delayed the enjambment
one beat or two too late
Called the world to care
about predestined fate
The world didn't listen

Had a bad day at work
Echoed Billy Collins
without benefit
of wit or experience

Had a bad day at work
Handwriting faltered
couldn't work the semi
from the colon

Bad day at work

Know when to keep your mouth shut
to climb down from your high horse
When to put it in the stable
and bolt the door

When you've walked in your enemy's shoes
and they still don't fit
cast them away
Always be comfortable in your own

Walk away from unrequited love
gently and without recrimination
Give more than you receive
The heart finds its equilibrium

Be kind

Sliding
on the pavement spittoon
frozen in winter
viscous in June

Between the slab cracks
fag dimps
cold chips

Lost souls
picking

For time to wander
slip-sodden streets
where the sun tips smiling hat
with last night's oil slicks weeping
read time well spent

Dead vermin undergrowth
the scent of moulding skins
of unrequited lust
power games lost
by bastards

Comical thrust of arms
blood pumped simmered veins
look foolish to nesting crows
(crows don't tell)

Bartok on the wireless
won't stop until the news
twenty minutes of scratching strings
designed for minds on pins

Attic lights light
for love or battle
dragging bones from beds of nails
bad friends' tittle-tattle

Rest in peace John Wesley

I'm under house arrest
for crimes against the Methodists

took a drink
enjoyed myself too much

Read erotic fiction
encouraged an erection and

had a cheeky bet
on some old nag

Wandered lost and lonely
on a horse, reflecting Wesley

on his lonesome quest
for misery and tears

found a home
ten miles away
in the age of horse
a chasm

won my bet

drowned in whisky

Cheers

Streetcar

After Orhan Veli Kanık (1914-1950), one of the founders of Türkiye's Garip Movement, which challenged formalistic rules, rhetoric and elaborate diction in the nation's poetry.

The patient by the window
in the deep pool winter's me

looking for my brothers
carousing on the street

Young Oktay and Melih
gossiping like children

about my kiss with Eleni
how I nipped a stranger's arse

my longing love for Catherine
the unrequited crush

my drinking indiscretions
that they made famous too

My room's so black it's purple
I want my brothers with me
holding out for middle age
in that streetcar of desire

I'm writing from the cwtsh
of my mini-palace
but suffering no exile
unlike Kaya, Nur or Hikmet

Some stare at my slim figure
you'd have thought me porcine
your cheekbones could slice fish
nibbled with your rakı
outside on the harbour
as the sun sank on Galata

I love your poem 'Gossip'
but prefer the name in Turkish
there's a bar named in its honour
in a small town that I love

Ministry of Fools

After 'Güzel Havalar' by Orhan Veli Kanık.

My job is soul destroying
days of shifting paper
working at the Ministry of Fools

Some say change is coming
While Adnan sits in prison
I still sit waiting, like I did at school

where the teachers didn't understand
my loving Father's legacy
hanging all around me like a noose

Tell Süreya I loved her
make the statement plain
not a lasting legacy I'd choose

Wherever you may be
you have a safe house with me

Backgammon games click
in the coffee house reception
where water turns rakı
to the milk of a lion

aslan sütü

I've wandered too far
from my safe house with you

Nuts

Three sharp rings
and a flat hello
Your mouth was full of nuts
you said

You swilled your teeth
in a pregnant pause
I thought of your imperfect mouth
sparkling in the bed

A strange town seldom visited

We tossed the talk
from watering plants
to weekends on our own

I thought of feelings cast in stone
Your mouth, my mind
nuts

Hello misty blue
It's been a while
since I thought of you

Five minutes are due
Too long
since I thought of you

Your left foot turned
quarter to nine
flat to the floor

Right hand on hip
slightly jutted

Occasionally amused
you bend at the waist
let the laughter fall

Your imperfect grin
allergic skin
you don't know what you started

Your face still damp from your undried hair
an echo of the sweat you wore on the brow
last night, as you sighed your first farewell
of our long goodbye
and our lives untwined

The freckles flecked on your parchment skin
I daren't breathe out as your sharp breath in
while my puckered lips meet an ice-cold screen
is a sign of lives detaching

Your fingertips on the gear stick
three hours before formed a human clutch
From then to now, everything you touch
gives me jealousy of objects

A five month stretch from the first flushed cheeks
the child-like thrill of a life's new bloom
to the sepia tint of a rented room
where the scent of last night lingers

My eyes could be hazel
blue, green or grey

You give nowt away

I've never been looked at
by brown eyes that way

In a dusky shade your shoes
bleed red
       Wedged and neatly tied
  Your left foot splayed   east

attracts the wrong attention
            Bent on ego
drawn to the colour not shade
            Splayed west

Test an acquaintance for
indifference
       Shrug from habit
formed young by your mother's early disappearance
       Tomatoes today

will flush your face
tomorrow
      The shade of my embarrassment

Your allergy to scarlet fruit
  My puce fear of you

It's as if she dies each night
that he gives way to speaking
charmless love-laden metaphors of
spite-spiked need

There's nothing remarkable about her
but her straight-edged ordinariness
Her refusal to be batted into the
21st century piffle of who cares most

about puking out the guts
of a Clinton Cards emotionally benign
super-charged sugar-loaded script

She shrugs
He heaves

Pulses never beating to the same tune
limbs always out of sync

She can't stop smiling
to keep it light, holding off his
insistence that there's something
where nothing ever lived

bar two nights of shy sex
and her hope that he would stop

stretching
for
affection

You are summer evenings
two glasses in

The whiff of herbs
cool terrace drinks

For my pain you are aspirin
for my burns, balm
for the thought I hurt you, honey
for my creeping madness, calm

He loves to leave you
in the early hours
when others stay

When he's with you
he's rarely rested
calm

He likes the drop
of the nearly sleeping moment
the hypnic jerk

falling from buildings
or stranded on top
during earthquakes

But you were never bedfellows
you left him on the shelf

while he is stalking others' dreams
you're fucking someone else

...and the gift he gave you
two weeks in
to each detail of your taste

was eaten square by square
with your slight half underbite

A speck of silver paper
catching on a filling

Disgust defined your look, like
each time he sent a message

Three weeks in you said

"Don't like that chocolate"

You're ungrateful as you're jagged

Jagged as your dancing

Moving at 11/8
to a standard
4/4 beat

Only the lonely
don't sing 'Only the Lonely'
even in the mirror
when the shaving bowl is tepid

Sleet winds howl outside
and last night's drinking
led to an unknown
body in bed

She left without a word
no shape or scent
just a faint sound as she went
chirping
"Only the lonely"

Don't sing that song

Only the lonely know
how he felt this morning
rasping regret
dry mouth yawning
front door clicking

We'll eat only vitamin pills
sculpt our faces on virtual screens
enter friendships on scores out of ten
leave them emotionless
but won't know quite when

Know when we're dying
to the nearest half day
appreciate living
in a Stepford Wives way

Cry only when ordered
laugh not at all
pay full disregard to the homeless

Make plans for living
without colour or joy

Hear soft shuffle footsteps
with no longing, regret
for her signature sound

The way that she left

On a planet somewhere distant
one of us considers –
digging out flower beds
asking the neighbours for a drink
joining a terrorist cell

When the improbable
chance of meeting comes
a traffic cop steps in
Right hand outstretched
as if managing the rush hour

Our polarity repels us
he didn't need to bother

Six degrees of separation

One too few for me

Yesterday
he burned your clothes on a pyre
Today
pretends that nobody knows
Tomorrow
commissions a statue of you

on a plinth in the bedroom
to help him get through
crafted of copper
by hands made of steel
with lips that are sealed
arms that are crossed

Once wooed by your feet
this statue's are lost
You stole time from working
in a bed in the Lakes
In a dull Midlands town
you turned love to heartbreak

You asked him to whistle
some troubadour's song
to keep you amused
while you strung him along
We all know that real men
are fearless and strong

The time was half right
The place was half wrong

A drayman's busman's holiday
A swift one at every stop

to ease aching bones
to smooth my way
from pub to pub
while I'm grafting

Precise punctuation
for each guttural pause

I could sup a sink or a bath-full
all the world's oceans and lakes
In your world of ultrasilence
this thirst is not for quenching

I don't want you because I want you
it's because you don't want me
The curse of poor reflective souls
since two thousand and twenty BC

It isn't the charm of your laughter
the sex, or the fall of your hair
'with love' birthday wishes
superfluous kisses

it's only that you don't care

There are just two causes I'd fight for
For one, I'll give you this oath

     Rejection is worse than bereavement
     Suicide a combination of both

Break-up album

Listening to your break-up album
a penny for your torture

a pound for each mention
that you're not drinking water

stumbling through club tables
bathed in booze and sweat

nobody is interested
in your drinking to forget

If I carry on
in sunshine
or marble-skied
Manchester

where clouds skip sadly
to the promise of
sometime sun

or the leap of joy
for the first swallow

or a tea-time pint
or two

I will think of you

for all time
blue

The alcoholic's prayer

'Found poems' are all the rage. So here's a lost one.

Give me whisky for my wounded heart
Brandy for my soul
Vodka to bring emptiness
Gin to fill that hole

Ale for when I'm sociable
Wine for when I'm not
Champagne for pretending
I'm something that I'm not

Absinthe to bring meaning
'though we haven't found it yet
and every drink that humans slug
to remember or forget

    I am an alcoholic
    My name is lost, I think
    I have no mind for detail
    when my head is in the drink

    I've neglected friends for memories
    lost love as regrets
    bad breath for an aura
    a hangman's stare for the hope that's left

    God told me to stop this thing
    It's the absinthe once again
    swapping creeping hopelessness
    for an imaginary friend

Paraffins

Early doors paraffins
the usual thing
Locals lower gaze
as old John shuffles in
with his arthritic hip
dribble down his chin
He drops half a crown
in the Marie Curie tin
decimal coinage never captured him
he sups electric bitter

The landlord looks grim
needs an ego trim
thinks he's charismatic
but he's just plain dim
Puts 10p on the bitter
waters down the gin
Used to be youthful
used to be slim
pretends he was in the Paras

Fat Phil cracks a joke
about those of other kin
claims he's not racist
excuses growing thin
best bloke in the world
if you've got the right skin

Log fire burned out
nights drawing in
watch out in the ginnel for migrants

The pilot light stays lit
the boiler unheated

Polish in the air
trumps bleach
greeting early doors lushes

Dave the postie's seat
sits empty
No two-thirty arrival
with racist views

No *Racing Post*
or *Evening News*

The seethe of the poppy debate
cools to a simmer

You've drunk too much
don't have another
You smoke too much
don't swear at your mother
For a hand he raised his voice instead
Now all of our fathers are dead

Shave with the grain
puff your cheeks out like this
Don't ask what that machine is
when we go for a piss
For a hand he raised a glass instead
Now all of our fathers are dead

Best ask your mother
Time for another
Put Sinatra on the wireless
Stop hitting your brother
Take me to the care home
Place a kiss on my head

Now all of our fathers are dead

Something that you said
"He can't come with us, he's dead"
stuck with me for decades
It still does

Your sister hoiked you shoulder-high
slung you on her back
We chattered to the local shop
bought Number 6 for old times

You mocked my endless misery
told me "Don't wear black"
In our retro table football game
played Norman Wisdom at left back

Then we built dry-stone walls
Setting the balance right
with chilblained hands

Tried to understand
wind-carried guttural Welsh
that mother thought crude

You went to war
I stayed at school

When dad was dying
you were ocean-bound
I picked the pieces up

You did your National Service
I worked in town
Sent cigarettes to Winnipeg

Now mum has strange moods
you didn't pick the pieces up
I don't want to be here at night

You were good with the kids
when they were young

Kite flying
Hamleys gifts at Christmas
crystallised fruit for Margaret

She's not well
the doctors can't explain
I'm losing my hair

We will visit Sunday

Next week we're moving north

Three foot by two
of chipboard and glue
this '80s fitted drawer
contains what's left of you

Your clothes now gone
some barely worn
I hope they keep some poor soul warm
in the unforgiving winter

You made no god of money
or had any gods at all

You wept at hopeless poverty
raged at pointless piety

wrapped your arms 'round family
and those in close proximity

Now this six-foot square enclosure
holds inconsequential objects

    A well-used comb, redundant now
        your two sons furrow balding brows
        scratch mirrored domes and wonder how
        you didn't pass that gene on

    A locket with an unknown face
        there's no one left to help us trace
        what her name was, her time or place
        in that faded generation

Gathered objects gather dust
mirrors tarnish
iron rusts

For all our hope
our love and lust
it's dust that we return to

We have things to make and do
paths to blindly follow
DIY to botch and cock
won't wait until tomorrow

Calculus continuum
algebraic formulae
wash the pots
darn your socks
make the fucking tea

The ladder steps we've climbed
the arses that we've kissed
regrets of books we've never read
epic films we've missed
faces never sculpted
the lack of lovers' trysts
measured SMART achievements
aspirational shopping lists

I thumb my nose at mission statements
and objective lists
despise business processes
I think you get the gist

I am neither born again
nor logical positivist
this tale has no pas de deux
pirouette or twist

I just like art galleries and getting pissed

flapjackpress.co.uk